The Middle Colonies
Breadbasket
of the New World

Kelly Rodgers

Consultants

Katie Blomquist
Fairfax County Public School

Nicholas Baker, Ed.D.
Supervisor of Curriculum and Instruction
Colonial School District, DE

Publishing Credits

Rachelle Cracchiolo, M.S.Ed., *Publisher*
Conni Medina, M.A.Ed., *Managing Editor*
Emily R. Smith, M.A.Ed., *Series Developer*
Diana Kenney, M.A.Ed., NBCT, *Content Director*
Johnson Nguyen, *Multimedia Designer*
Lynette Ordoñez, *Editor*

Image Credits: Cover, p. 1 LOC [LC-USZC4-12141]; pp. 2–3, 5–7, 9–11, 13, 15–18, 21, 23–27, 32 North Wind Picture Archives; pp. 4, 25 Granger, NYC; pp. 7, 31 National Archive; p. 8 LOC [LC-DIG-pga-01466]; p. 9 LOC [LC-USZC4-12217]; p. 11 Daderot/Wikimedia Commons/CC0 1.0; pp. 12–13 LOC [DIG-ppmsca-31798]; p. 14 Pictorial Press Ltd/Alamy; p. 20 Ted Spiegel/CORBIS; p. 22 National Museum of African American History and Culture/Smithsonian; p. 27 Encyclopedia Britannica/LOC; p. 28 LOC [LC-USZC4-12141]; p. 29 LOC [vc006399]; all other images from iStock and/or Shutterstock.

Library of Congress Cataloging-in-Publication Data

Names: Rodgers, Kelly, author.
Title: The middle colonies : breadbasket of the New World / Kelly Rodgers.
Description: Huntington Beach, CA : Teacher Created Materials, 2016. | Includes index. | Audience: Grades 4-6.?
Identifiers: LCCN 2015051146 | ISBN 9781493830763 (pbk.)
Subjects: LCSH: Middle Atlantic States--History--Colonial period, ca. 1600-1775--Juvenile literature.
Classification: LCC F106 .R746 2016 | DDC 974/.02--dc23
LC record available at http://lccn.loc.gov/2015051146

Teacher Created Materials
5301 Oceanus Drive
Huntington Beach, CA 92649-1030
http://www.tcmpub.com
ISBN 978-1-4938-3076-3

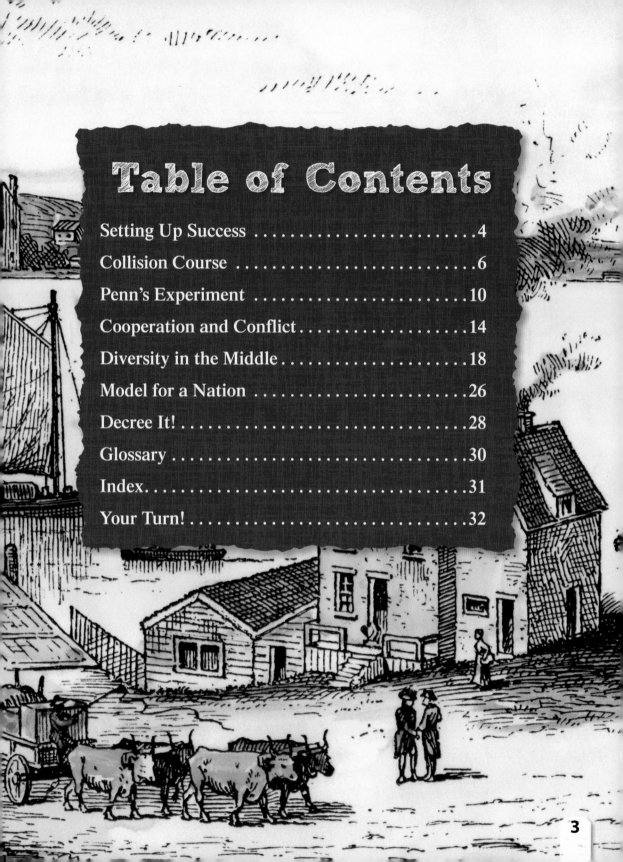

Table of Contents

Setting Up Success

In the 1500s and 1600s, the English established colonies in the **New World**. Families who wanted to practice their religion freely set up colonies in the north. They worked in the lumber and the shipbuilding industries. In the south, men built colonies in hopes of getting rich. Large farms were key to their success. But the English wanted to control the whole east coast. They set their sights on the middle colonies.

The middle colonies were started by people from the Netherlands, or the Dutch. They had no idea that their colonies would become such a success. People came to live there for many reasons. These people came from different backgrounds. The middle colonies became the most **diverse** colonies. They grew and **prospered**. As they did, they helped set a standard for what would later become a new nation.

Dutch settlers in New Netherland

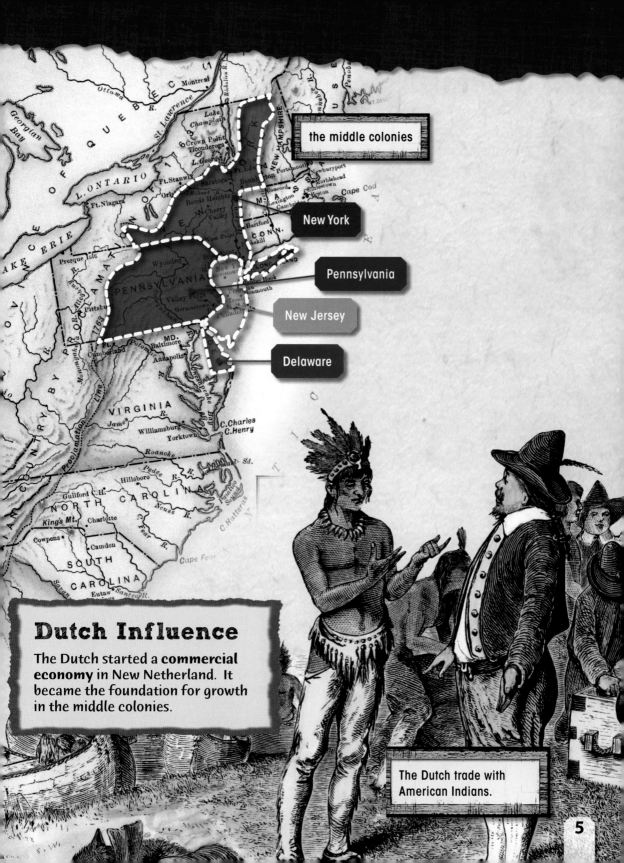

the middle colonies

New York

Pennsylvania

New Jersey

Delaware

Dutch Influence

The Dutch started a **commercial economy** in New Netherland. It became the foundation for growth in the middle colonies.

The Dutch trade with American Indians.

Collision Course

The story of the middle colonies begins with Henry Hudson. He was an explorer who worked for the Dutch. In 1609, he was searching for a way to reach Asia by traveling through the Arctic Ocean. But his path was blocked with ice. He turned around and sailed across the Atlantic Ocean instead. He thought a waterway across North America might be the answer. He found a broad, flat river. So he claimed the land along the river for the Dutch. There, the Dutch developed a colony called New Netherland.

The Dutch had not found a **Northwest Passage** to Asia. But they did start a fur trading business. They established New Amsterdam. It became the capital of New Netherland. Sweden and Finland had built colonies on the Delaware River. The Dutch took over those colonies, too.

Henry Hudson's ship, *Half-Moon*, leaves for the New World in 1609.

The fur trade was **profitable**. But few Dutch families wanted to go to the New World. So the Dutch invited settlers from other countries to their new colony. People from all over Europe moved to the Dutch colony.

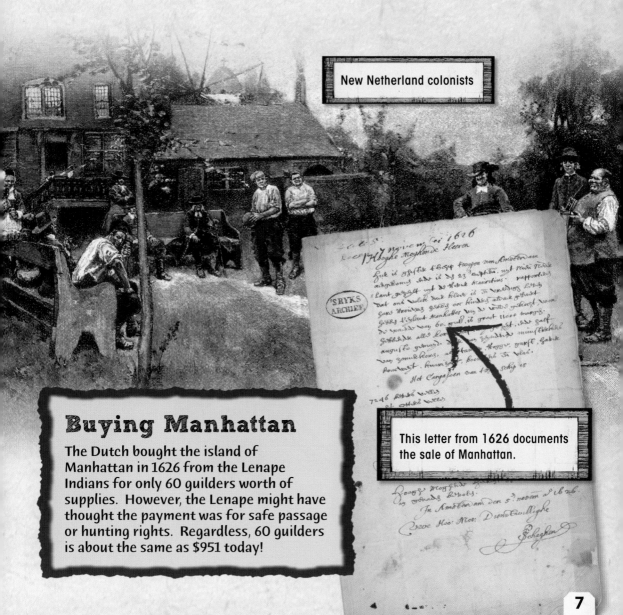

New Netherland colonists

This letter from 1626 documents the sale of Manhattan.

Buying Manhattan

The Dutch bought the island of Manhattan in 1626 from the Lenape Indians for only 60 guilders worth of supplies. However, the Lenape might have thought the payment was for safe passage or hunting rights. Regardless, 60 guilders is about the same as $951 today!

The English were making money from their colonies. But they wanted to make more. They did not like that the Dutch colony separated their New England from their southern colonies. The two countries wanted wealth and power. They wanted to build **empires**. They were on a **collision** course.

In 1664, King Charles II of England made a plan with his brother. His brother was James, the Duke of York. They planned to force the Dutch out of North America. They sent 300 to 450 soldiers to New Amsterdam. They were prepared to fight the Dutch for the colony. But the Dutch surrendered. Not a single shot was fired. The English took the colony. They renamed it New York and the capital New York City.

Later, the king gave the southern portion of the colony to two friends. It became a new colony known as New Jersey. Land there was offered for sale. Settlers were promised religious freedom. Both New York and New Jersey attracted more settlers.

The English take over New Amsterdam in 1664.

New Jersey Colony

The colonists who settled in New Jersey **cooperated** with the American Indians. It became known as a tolerant and peaceful colony.

Choosing to Surrender

Peter Stuyvesant (STY-vuh-suhnt) was **governor** of New Netherland. When the English arrived to take the colony, he wanted to fight. The settlers refused.

Dutch colonists beg the governor not to fire on English ships.

Penn's Experiment

Soon, another colony was founded in the middle region. It was created with a **land grant** from the king of England. William Penn's family had loaned money to King Charles II. The king repaid them with a gift. In 1681, he gave them a large piece of land in North America along the Delaware River.

Penn was a Quaker. The Quakers were a religious group that had faced **persecution** in England. They had their own beliefs. Quakers worshipped without ministers. And women were allowed to be church leaders. Quakers also refused to fight in wars. Some people thought Quakers were a threat. Penn wanted to build a place in the New World for the Quakers. There, they could practice their religion freely.

Penn's colony would not ban different religions like others did. People of all religions were welcomed. All who wanted to work hard for a successful life in the New World were invited to Penn's Woods. The new colony was called Pennsylvania (pen-suhl-VEYN-yuh).

William Penn

Puritans

The Puritans also sought religious freedom in the colonies. They settled in New England, north of the middle colonies. They did not allow people with other religions in their colonies.

Word spread quickly. By 1686, Penn's colony had 8,000 people. It was the fastest growing English colony. **Merchants** and **artisans** came to settle the land. Farmers came, too. The growing season was longer than that of New England. And the soil was rich and fertile. Farmers grew wheat and other grains. They were able to grow more food than they needed. So they sold their crops to others.

A city named Philadelphia came to life. *Philadelphia* means "city of brotherly love." Penn helped design this park-like city. There were wide streets and city squares. It became a large port city. Its merchants found success in trade and became the richest in the colonies.

Penn's land grant also included the former New Sweden colony on the Delaware River. The region south of the river was given its own assembly in 1704. This was its governing body. But it was still part of Pennsylvania until 1776.

Philadelphia port

Delaware Turnover

Delaware was founded by the Swedish in 1638. It was taken over by the Dutch in 1655. The English controlled it after the Dutch surrendered. Then, it was part of Penn's land grant. It was part of Pennsylvania until it officially split off in 1776.

Cooperation and Conflict

American Indians lived on the land that became the middle colonies for thousands of years. Before settlers had arrived, five tribes formed a pact, or an agreement. They called it the Iroquois (EER-uh-kwoy) Confederacy. The pact was made to help keep peace among the tribes. A council of chiefs met to talk about problems. They made decisions together.

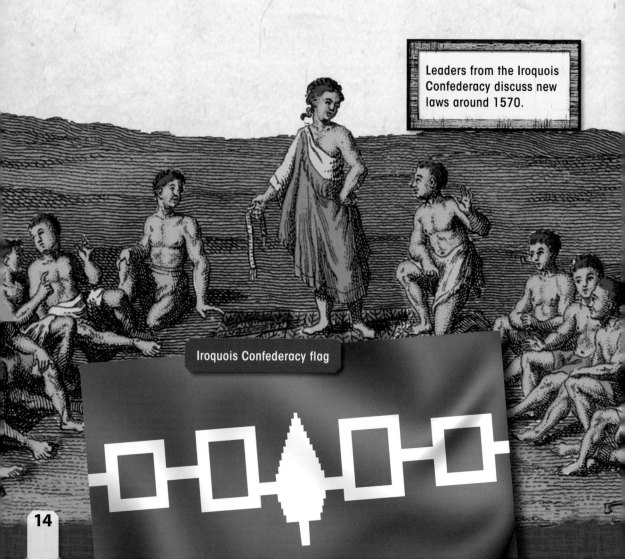

Leaders from the Iroquois Confederacy discuss new laws around 1570.

Iroquois Confederacy flag

Fur traders talk with American Indians.

Then, the Europeans arrived. The Iroquois knew they would have to work with them. They hoped they could hold onto their land. They hoped they could live the way they always had. The Dutch tried to cooperate with the Iroquois. The Dutch wanted help in the fur trade. But the English were less willing. They were not sure colonists and American Indians could live side by side peacefully. The English thought their ways of life were too different. When the English took control of New Netherland, they agreed to cooperate. But as more colonists arrived, they wanted more land. Promises were broken. Settlers took land without permission.

Inspiration

The Iroquois Confederacy had an unwritten constitution. It explained membership rights, roles, and organization. This constitution may have influenced Benjamin Franklin's thoughts about the new American government.

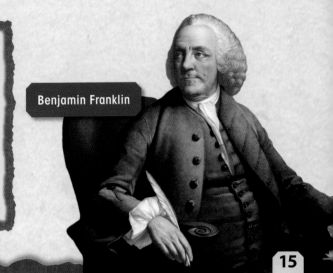

Benjamin Franklin

William Penn wanted things to be different in Pennsylvania. He learned lessons from other colonies. His Quaker beliefs helped, too. Penn thought that friendly relationships were key. He reached out to the Lenni Lenape tribe before he came to North America. He wrote a letter to their leader. In the letter, Penn said that he had love and respect for the Lenni Lenape. He said they were the true owners of the land. He wrote that he hoped to gain their trust. He promised to be honest and peaceful. He said his settlers would be, too.

Penn makes a treaty with American Indians.

Penn kept his word. He allowed colonists to settle only on land they paid for. They paid fair prices for the land. He made courts that settled disputes fairly. Tribes in other colonies came to Pennsylvania. There, they could escape harsh treatment. For more than 50 years, colonists and American Indians lived peacefully in Pennsylvania.

Diversity in the Middle

The king of England hoped the middle colonies would help him create a large empire in North America. He hoped people would speak the same language. He thought they would have the same values. But something else happened. The middle colonies became the most diverse of all.

Swedish settlers in the middle colonies

Religious Tolerance

Settlers from many countries came to the middle colonies. They were from Germany and the Netherlands. They were from Sweden, Ireland, and England. People were from Africa, too. People brought their own customs and ways of life. They had their own languages. They had their own religions.

Life changed in the middle colonies. Settlers did not make their own countries. They learned to live together. Many had come to the middle colonies for religious freedom. Once there, they practiced religious tolerance. They let others practice their own religions. No one faith became the most powerful. This later became a key part of a new American identity.

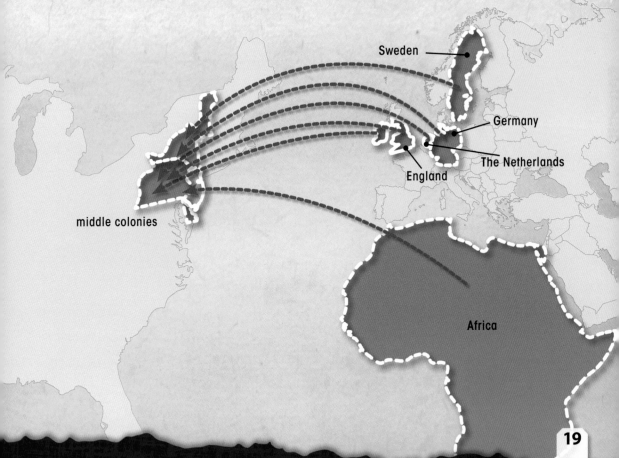

Sweden

Germany

The Netherlands

England

middle colonies

Africa

Farmers and Merchants

The middle colonies were created with land grants. Their purpose was to make money for the owners of the land and the king. The economy of the middle colonies grew strong. Farmers grew wheat, barley, corn, rye, and flax. They raised cattle and pigs. Farmers grew so much food that they had plenty to sell. The middle colonies fed colonists all over North America. They became known as the breadbasket of the New World.

A commercial economy developed, too. Sawmills produced lumber. Wheat grinders made flour. People built ships and mined iron. Wide rivers made trade easier. Merchants and farmers could easily move their products to the coast. New York City and Philadelphia became great port cities. The colonies prospered.

Farmers in the middle colonies used animals to help them plow fields, as seen here.

Politics in the Middle

Each colony had its own governor and legislature. Each legislature had two houses, or groups. The governor chose men for the upper house. The people elected men to serve in the lower house. Only men could vote. And only men could be elected. These two houses worked together to make laws. But the governor or the king could reject any law he did not like.

Port of New Amsterdam in 1667

An Earned Reputation

Colonists grew many grains, such as wheat, rye, barley, and oats. They also grew pumpkins, squash, and beans of all types. This bounty of food helped them earn their reputation for being the breadbasket of the New World.

Africans and Slavery

Colonists brought Africans to the middle colonies to work for them. At first, colonists brought them as **indentured servants**. This meant they were sometimes freed after they worked for a period of time. But soon, colonists began bringing Africans over as slaves. A slave is a person who is owned by another. Slave owners forced slaves to work for them without pay. Slaves had no freedom. Slaves in the middle colonies were usually forced to do household work. They were also coachmen and cooks. But they were not paid for the work they did.

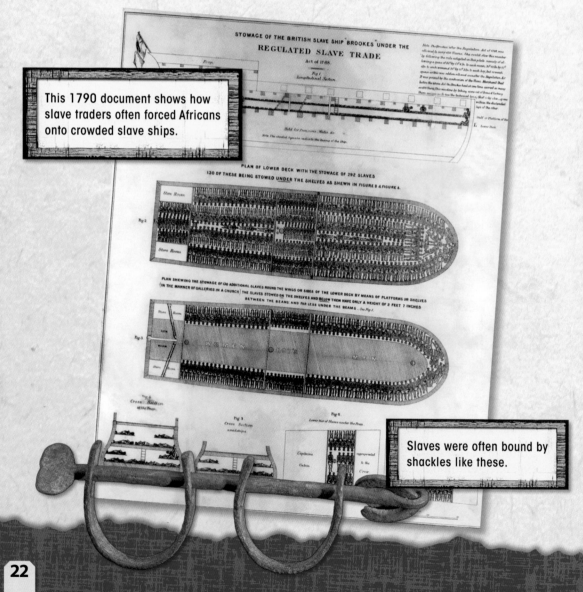

This 1790 document shows how slave traders often forced Africans onto crowded slave ships.

Slaves were often bound by shackles like these.

Indentured servants and slaves had difficult lives. Africans were not thought of as equal to white colonists. They did not have the same rights. But colonists treated slaves the worst. They didn't allow slaves to gather in groups. Slaves weren't allowed to carry weapons. And there were no laws to protect them from cruel punishments.

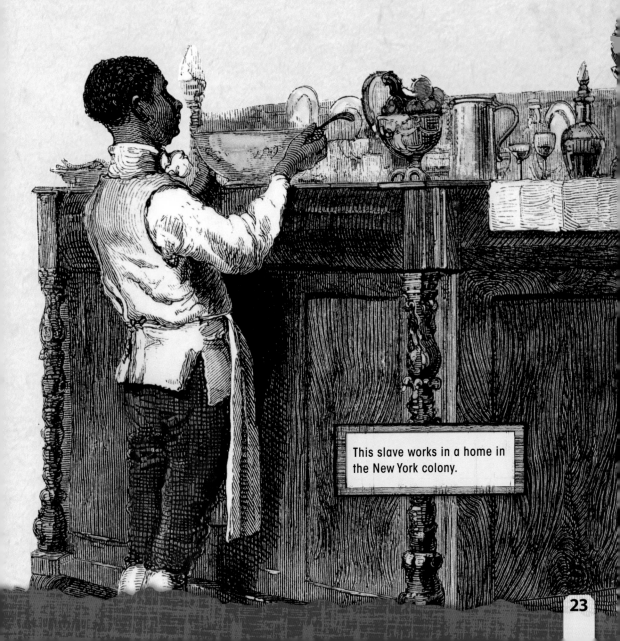

This slave works in a home in the New York colony.

Family Life

Colonial families worked hard. They often had eight to ten children. Though sometimes, children did not live to adulthood. Each family member had an important role. Men ran farms and businesses. Women cared for the children. They took care of the home, and they worked on family farms, too. Girls worked alongside their mothers. Boys often served **apprenticeships** to learn trades. Most social activities centered around religion.

Everyone worked from sunup to sundown. Farm life revolved around the seasons. There was always work to be done. Crops were planted in the spring. Farmers tended their crops in the summer. Crops were harvested in the fall. In the winter, plans were made for the next spring.

Swedish settlers farm along the Delaware River.

Farmhouses were often cold and dark. Candles and fireplaces were the only sources of light. In the winter months, homes were heated by fire. Often, sickness swept through communities. Diseases killed hundreds. There were few doctors. Most received little formal training. In 1765, the first medical college was founded in Philadelphia. This helped people get the care they needed.

A young girl peels apples.

This 1726 book describes smallpox in the colonies.

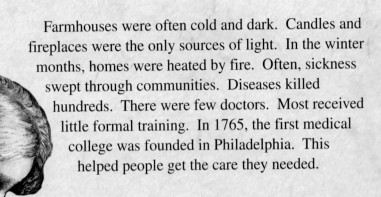

An Historical

ACCOUNT

OF THE

SMALL-POX

INOCULATED

IN

NEW ENGLAND,

Upon all Sorts of Persons, *Whites, Blacks,* and of all Ages and Constitutions.

With some Account of the Nature of the Infection in the NATURAL and INOCULATED Way, and their different Effects on HUMAN BODIES.

With some short DIRECTIONS to the UNEXPERIENCED in this Method of Practice.

Humbly dedicated to her Royal Highness the Princess of WALES, by *Zabdiel Boylston,* Physician.

LONDON:

Printed for S. CHANDLER, at the Cross-Keys in the Poultry, M.DCC.XXVI.

Deadly Virus

The smallpox virus killed many people. Along with fever and vomiting, smallpox caused people to break out in painful pus-filled blisters and scabs.

Model for a Nation

In many ways, the middle colonies served as a model for a new American nation. A diverse group of people settled there. As a result, a diverse society arose. No one group was in control. The people who lived there were different in many ways. This made them more accepting of others. They did not have to be the same to get along. So the middle colonies became a great success. The people worked hard. Businesses thrived and cities grew.

For a long time, England left the colonists on their own. They believed the colonists were working to help the **mother country**. But the region's diversity meant that England was not the mother country for everyone. Colonists thought they should benefit from their own hard work—not a country and king across the sea. They wanted more freedom. They wanted to make their own decisions. These differences would create conflict. Conflict would turn to war. And soon a new nation would emerge, founded largely on the ideals of the middle colonies.

New York in the 1700s

Freedom of the Press

Even before the First Amendment, the middle colonies supported freedom of the press. In 1733, John Peter Zenger wrote about a corrupt governor, William Cosby, in the *New-York Weekly Journal*. Zenger was put in jail for it. During his trial (pictured above), the stories were proven true. Zenger was released.

Decree It!

The middle colonists elected men to make laws for them. Laws serve several purposes. They help keep the peace and maintain order. Laws help people settle conflicts and disputes. Laws can also protect people's rights.

If you were a middle colonist, what laws would you want in your colony? Remember that people from many countries are your neighbors. These people may have different beliefs and ways of life. And American Indians lived on this land long before you arrived. Write at least five laws you would want in your colony.

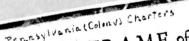

Pennsylvania (Colony) Charters

The FRAME of the

GOVERNMEN

OF THE

Province of Pennsilvania

IN

AMERICA:

Together with certain

LAWS

Agreed upon in England

BY THE

GOVERNOUR

AND

Divers FREE-MEN of the aforesaid

PROVINCE.

To be further Explained and Confirmed there by the firſt
Provincial Council and *General Aſſembly* that ſhall
be held, if they ſee meet.

Printed in the Year MDCLXXXII.

This document lays out how Pennsylvania will be governed. As in other documents around this time, some of the *s*'s look like *f*'s.

Glossary

apprenticeships—positions in which a person is taught a trade by a skilled worker

artisans—people who are skilled at making things by hand

collision—a crash in which two or more people or objects hit each other

commercial economy—a system in which goods and services have monetary values

cooperated—worked together to do something

diverse—made up of people or things that are different from one another

empires—groups of countries that are controlled by one ruler

governor—a person who is the leader of a region

indentured servants—people who work for others to earn their freedom or property

land grant—a contract that gives ownership of a plot of land

merchants—people who buy and sell goods for money

mother country—the original country where colonists came from

New World—the western hemisphere of the world; especially North, Central, and South America

Northwest Passage—a sea route connecting the Atlantic and Pacific Oceans along the northern coast of America

persecution—the unfair treatment of someone because of their beliefs

profitable—able to make money

prospered—became successful usually by making money

Index

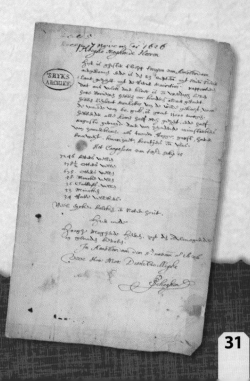

Life in the Middle Colonies

This is an engraving from the 1800s. It shows the middle colonies in the 1600s. How did people in the 1800s see life in the middle colonies? How does this image support the idea that the middle colonies were the breadbasket of the New World? Write a paragraph to answer these questions.